In January and June

By Olivia Kaye

Sadlier-Oxford
A Division of William H. Sadlier, Inc.

In January I wear
a jacket and jeans.

In June I wear
a T-shirt and shorts.

In January I jump
in the snow.

In June I jump
in the water.

In January I play jacks
with my sister.

In June I play ball
with my sister.

But I eat peanut butter
and jelly all year round!